Winged Words

Annette Elizabeth Sykes

I would like to dedicate this volume of Winged Words, to my family who have given me the opportunity to express myself in poetry and to my Husband, Graham who has supported me wholeheartedly through my wildest imaginings and creative meltdowns during our long and happy marriage. Also to Rosemary Drewery who was the final instigator in allowing this book to be born.

Table of Contents

Spirit Of Night

As darkness creeps unhindered
Staining the sky with washes of indigo,
Drowning the earths' joyous palette
As a writers, ink might spill and seep
Through each cell, it encounters.

The world stills, pauses awhile, then
Emergence of strength,
Emergence of power,
Spirit of night awakes,
Protecting the slumbers of innocents
Old and young alike.

Prancing through our dreams
Protecting us 'til dawns' watercolour
Of freshly mixed pigments
Glazes the indigo in muted light.

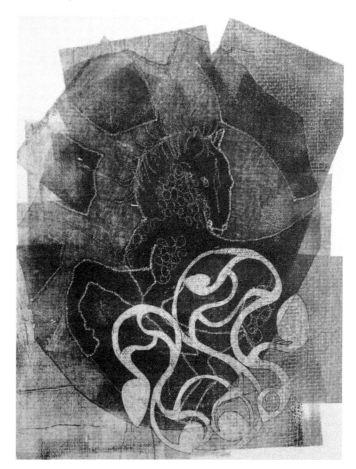

Gone Fishing

Elegant grey morning attire,
Enhanced by creamy breast,
Long legs emerge from a streamlined chest.
Aloof stance, strutting with infinite care.
Statue stillness, barely a feather stirs,
Only displaced by the slightest breeze
Ruffling his formal dress.

Long spear-like pointed beak
Angling in readiness for the slightest splash
Of an unsuspecting finned and tailed bleak.
A tasty morsel tossed and turned in a flash.

An adversary appears from between the reeds,
But no rabble behaviour here proceeds.
Propriety prevails, they each keep their poise
And continue to fish in their own solitary pools.

The Fisherman True

Gnarled blackened posts, smoothed by wear.
Sculpted; riven by chain and fray.
Standing as sentinels to a living, breathing quay,
Reminders of industry, fishing and brew.
Forgotten now, except by a few,
Who keep its 'secrets hugged so tight,
This secluded spot so silent day and night.
A haven for the sweet violets
Which busily occupy the vacant site.

So, too, for the fish who now
Without pollution, flourish and grow,
Attracting the attention of a fisherman true.
The tern who swoops and swerves so low,
Calling the while in a haunting refrain,
Dives and returns, again and again,
Until, at last, efforts rewarded
He retires to enjoy his hard-won gain.

3

Arianrhod

With silver thread so fine,
She weaves to her will
Elements of cosmic space and
time.

Drumming, thrumming from
deepest blue,
Infinite forces now combine,
Creating life from stuff sublime
Shape and form, re-arrange and
renew
And from her hands, her creation
flew.

Moon Goddess

As old and wise as time she stands,
Untouched, it seems, by eons hand.

The burgeoning moon with arms
outstretched.
She greets with ritual forever
etched,
Upon mists of times constant repeat,
Cycle of lune again complete.

Moonglow

Ages past have left no trace.
Of time upon her beauteous face,
Lifted up to greet the moon,
Secrets hugged to internal tune.
Delights to be savoured every night,
As moonglow transforms dark to light.

Shadowy lives beyond our reach,
Legends of stones are there to teach.
Stories abound, faery and folklore,
Round every corner of our ancient shore.

The Vast Void

Darkness, stillness,
The vast void of nothing
Echoing through my mind,
Stretching into the universal zero.
Midnight dark, soft and seductive as velvet,
Infinitely wrapping me in its 'arms.

Self-melting, dissolving, dissembling into the ether.
Shape and form morphing into emptiness
As a redundant, discarded vessel;
Touching nothing, everything, all and all.

Bass, thrumming, vibrating sounds,
Birthing at the deepest core.
Slamming into the vacuum as if it were a wall, Displacing atoms into invisible patterns.

Worlds of rock vying for space,

Create writings in the void,
Energetic imprints, a sound so vast,

Beyond imagining. Beyond experience?

Wondrous tendrils creeping into my mind,
Comprehension dawning, instantly retreating.
Leaving behind questioning impressions,
Mortality returns, yet nothing, nothing,
Ever to be the same.

And So The Spirit Flies

Have you ever had an experience so weird and wonderful that it takes your breath away and sends you scuttling into your inner world of creation?
This piece of work is the result of one such moment, and although not finished yet, it was calling to be shared even in its' infancy.
It is as if it just cannot wait to be born and be shared with you all, so here she is evolving as we travel to fruition together.

It was a surreal night of hustle and bustle, sirens and blue lights, slowing down, voices hushed in respect for the unexpected passing of a friend and neighbour of many years.

So it was a very bleary-eyed me who emerged the next day into the icy blast of a February morning with my black lab, Vinnie.

I had barely reached the bottom of the driveway when I heard the unmistakable whirring of wings. 'No, it can't be impossible', but sure enough, there they were, a pair of white swans powering along in their grace and beauty. Now, this might not seem unusual to you, but I cross my heart, in all the years I have lived here, never have I seen swans in my particular patch of sky – and I am an avid observer of anything avian!

But there they were, and I stood in awe, watching with bated breath as they flew low over the home opposite, then amazingly circled around over me before disappearing across the fields.

A single white feather floated down.
Swans mate for life and if you have ever had the privilege of watching their courtship, you will know that it is so intricate, tender and intimate that you feel like an intruder, a voyeur upon their privacy. They are completely 'into' each other and oblivious of all else. They symbolise eternal love and partners for life, which is what this couple were, devoted to each other and their two daughters.

Now call me whimsical if you like, but to me it meant only one thing and the title tells it all, 'And So The Spirit Flies'.

As I walked on, I noticed the purest of snowdrops nodding their brave acquiescence in the biting cold of a winter morn. They seemed to have popped up overnight, there were so many of them.

Do you know the story around their symbolism?

According to classicism, when Eve shed tears as she was banished from Eden, an angel picked up a snowflake and tossed it up into the air to make her smile; the snowflake shattered as it fell and became a snowdrop, a symbol of new beginnings and hope.

Thus they play an important part in my imagery, symbolising innocence, hope, sympathy and rebirth.

All day, these images played over and over in my head and heart, almost too overwhelming for me to actually begin the process of putting anything down, but it was so insistent that I had to begin.

I found a big board, 30 x 24 inches and began, gesso, texture, print, then out came the sewing machine.
I have never been so sure and swift in my work, she was just meant to be!
I hope you love her, she has opened doors to emotion and positivity I could only have dreamed of last week, so sad that it took a loss to make it so.

Red Kite

With elbowed wings upturned to the fingers
Like an expertly tautened bow
And forked tail directionally tilting,
He rides the invisible currents,
Rising, rising, higher to go.

As a master mariner tames the temperate tides,
He unerringly reads the invisible flow,
Choosing as instinct dictates, a thermal to glide,
Rising, rising, higher to go.

Space

Tiny indents in the ceaseless chatter
Within and without.
Silent moments between crochet and quaver,
Extension of waiting, prolonging the gap,
A precious time to take a chance
And peep into the energetic dance
Behind the curtain which veils our mind.

A sliver of space is all we need,
No longer games of the mind to heed;
Just slip through the chink, then 'Hark',
The miracle that lurks in the midnight dark,
Reveals to those who seek quiet solace.

Masked by myth and spurious magic,
Twined since eternity in learning and logic;
Our Source awaits, a shining lark,

Arising in song from the infinite dark.
Our own self there to be found,

The key is space, silence unbound.

Brushing Up

These busy, dashing birds in black, orange and white;
The vision of seabird personified. Inspiration, a designer's delight.

In dinner suits, they trot
Betwixt shallows and rock,
To prise and probe for whelk or cockle.
Orange legs burnished to match the bill,
Eyes made up, too; dressed to kill.

Pausing here, splashing there,
Constantly preening the feathers.
Brushing up all the while,
Allowing me, the viewer, a constant smile.

Trawling the shoreline for morsels sweet,
They shuffle en masse to the end of the beach.
Then, as one at a call, they all take flight,
A flock of striped wings in black and white.

And So the Spirit Soars

How many of us have experienced the gut-wrenching, heartbreaking pain of losing a fur baby, our loyal, unconditionally loving companion?

Then you will know how I felt when our black Labrador, Vinnie, who was admittedly old and wobbly (13) but still happy and wagging, suddenly had to be put to sleep last week. Something we sign up for when we fall in love, yet we still put ourselves through it.
He had spent the last few days acting like a 5-year-old, chasing the grandkids puppy around. We were politely informed by our 6-year-old, Kate, that the pup was; 'Having her period!'

Well, what fun and games. I am sure that you can conjure up the scene: 6-month-old Border Terrier, 13-year-old black Lab, talk about the 'spirit is willing' and all that!

Hence, Vinnies' bed had to be moved into our bedroom - on the ground floor, stairs were abandoned ages ago!

That morning, I awoke to a cold nose and imploring eyes - 'Wake up, Mum' We had a little walk and another chase of the pup, and all seemed as good as could be - albeit deaf and going a little 'cuckoo' occasionally.

Then, the nightmare, what we all signed up for, came to fruition. The time had come as he suddenly began to cough up bright, fresh blood.

The 100-mile dash to our vet seemed like a thousand, but they were waiting when we made it.

I cuddled him and he gazed directly into my eyes as he dimmed; as his eyes closed for the last time, I howled; no other word for it, I howled, husband with tears streaming down his face. At this very moment a Red Kite, high in the blue yonder, screamed as if echoing our anguish as a life so treasured extinguished.

As I am sure you know, all the platitudes in the world, like "you did the right thing," etc., just don't cut it, you just want to nurse that pain until it is ready to go.

And so it was, we brought him home - to a house which now feels empty and soulless, clean, but so quiet and empty.

Wrapped in his bubbly mat and with his grey 'Wabbit' by his side, we laid him tenderly to rest in his favourite woodland area amongst the primroses, which later on will be joined by nodding masses of bluebells.

This writing and this piece of work, 'And the Spirit Soared,' has been so cathartic and is a tribute to a beautiful, gentle companion and furry family member whose love and memories will stay in my heart forever.

Jump For Joy

The dark and brutal cold
Fields frozen into rock,
Trees, fingers of ice, so cold.
Feathers and fur fluffed to the fullest extent,
Watches with bated breath
Winters' eerie portent.
As beneath the fairy flakes of snow
Earth huddles under nature's winter blanket,
Secrets, wrapped and hidden, await to grow.

At last, a sigh, a deep exhale,
The slumbering land awakes,
As nature finally relinquishes its' delicate veil.
Life, at last, peeks expectant and coy,
And as it weaves its' eternal magic,
The horse, in its' element, jumps for joy.

Pools Of Solitude

Sitting alone in my pool of solitude,
Heart wrenched in two.
Caught between their worlds,
As the busy carousel of life
Grinds its 'noisy, giddy way
Round and round,
Escaping all thought, all feeling
Within its 'gaudy, cheerfulness.

Surface jollity, hiding in the light,
The glaring spotlight of life.
Beneath, the fragile veil rents,
Drowning, tears escaping,
As I crawl into the kindliness
Of the dark shadows
To lick my wounds
In my own pool of solitude.

The Ties That Bind

Oh, how strong are the ties that bind?
A silken thread,
A cobweb spun so fine?
An invisible cord that you will only find
Within your heart and mind.

Yet strong, long and flexible as steel,
Unbreakable,
Even in death.
Parent, child, lover; only you will feel
The tightening when they begin to unreel.

But, let them go, as a bird in flight,
Freedom, they think
Is what they desire.
But the ties truly are too tight.
The ribbons that bind will repair in hindsight.

Gifted

The rainbow of life brought each one of you down
Into our lives,
Perfect and beautiful.
Each is different and individual.

The touch of tiny fingers, almost forgotten,
Smiles, real or imagined.
Grasping life seemingly so frail
Belied by voices so hearty and hale.

Grandchildren grow and give so much pleasure,
Kisses and cuddles,
Laughter and fun with us to be found
Like the carousel of life, love keeps going round.

Gift is a word often bandied about,
Parcels, presents,
Colourful wrapping.
But to us, the gift is so much greater,
Our love for you all is treasured beyond measure.

New Adventures

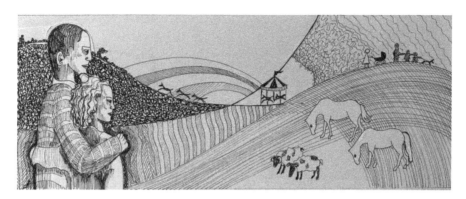

New adventures, it seems,
Is what they desire;
'Pastures anew', comes to mind;
Not caring or thinking about what they leave behind.

The roundabout turns yet again,
Disgorging its 'carefree riders
Where it will, serendipity coercing with fate,
Combining forces, a new life to create.

Children borrowed for a while,
Orbit us, as stars in their firmament,
Never meant to be a fixture permanent.
Independence encouraged with love and a smile,
Always taught to brave the extra mile.

Foolishness or bravura, no one can tell,
But the tear in the heart signs a job done well;
No fear of change in their short lives,
Home is now a moveable feast,
Including us out, a double-edged beast.

For My Grandson

At Grandma's'house, I have beautiful dreams,
Wrapped up in swathes of blues and greens.
Sunlit days, dappled light,
Sweet dreams are assured every night.

The bath all to myself, then story time;
My own choice of book every time.
The cosiest of beds, the warmest of quilts,
Snuggling down, wrapped up to the hilt.

Big Ted guarding the side of the bed,
Ellies one, two and three lined up by my head.
Gramps, big and round, sat by my side,
The comfiest cushion in the whole worldwide.

Comforting sounds of family around,
Coax me into a sleep so sound.
Dawn creeps along, then morning beams,
At Grandma's house I have beautiful dreams.

Moonshadows

A huge white moon, full and fit to burst,
Hanging heavily over the frost-silvered trees,
Creating long elegant moon shadows across the twinkling glade.

Morning still has sleep in its' solemn eyes
As my footsteps crunch up the grassy hill,
Leaving tell-tale spoor like an individual fingerprint,
Signing my wandering route for those with eyes to see.

Pink Morn bursts triumphantly across the sky,
Colours splashed like radiant paint,
Coaxing diamond sparkles from leaves and branches,
Coating the livestock with gentling rosy dawn.

Dog panting, excitedly scampering,
Droplets of pearl on whiskers and breath.
Light creeping into the hollows and hedges,
Lifting hidden pockets of low-lying mist.

And gradually looming up from the gloaming half-light,
Wonderful gnarled and twisted trees,
Standing like ancient sentinels
At the borders of our worlds,
Protecting us with huge spreading boughs
Woven with dripping ivy and lush, soft moss.

I stand at the crest of the hill, watching in wonder
As the sun's rays race across the somnolent landscape,
Devouring greedily the soft pre-dawn,
Banishing the mysterious, mystical moon shadows
Until eventide, when the sun's battle is lost
And darkness returns to reign again.

The Pipe of Skeldro

The pipe of Skeldro
Joins with the plaintive cry
Of the Whaup,
Yet whipped away
By the howling ferocity
Of wind and rain.

And beneath the dark
And scudding pall,
The sheltering fledglings huddle
In peaty bog
And densely beflowered plain.

A Flicker of Ghost Grey

A flicker of ghost grey from the corner of the eye,
The hush of cashmere-soft feathers
Tilting to catch the slightest draught.

A plaintive cry, haunting the darkly lit
Hiding places of its 'trembling prey.

A sudden stall, a silent swoop,
Finely honed talons close like iron.

A soft, furry body so swiftly limp,
Even the whispering grasses seem to
Bow their heads in respect.

A Contact Point

Pain, a contact point,
Physical meeting spiritual.
Grinding, graunching, debilitating pain.
But all as intended,
All in perfect alignment
With the infallible order
Of the universal template.

Giving the gift of solitude,
Blessed relief from harried life,
Time to think, time to reflect,
Contemplation the reward
Of self-respect.

As iron is tempered by heat and cold,
Character forged in flames untold,
Flesh so soft and weak at birth
Matures and mellows as a tree of great
girth.
'Baptism of fire' some would quote,
Quenched in due course,
Thro' acceptance to devote
The respite was thus given,
To thought, creation and this poem, thus written.

Angels

Drifting, drifting gently down,
Curling light, soft as down,
White as snow as it touches the ground.
A tiny feather, perfectly formed,
A gift from a being angel born.

Or shimmering, glimmering in the night,
There beside us, an angel or two
With wings of changing ethereal hue.
Shifting, lifting, lightening the dark,
Open your mind, your ears, your heart.
The lightest touch and, yes, 'Hark.'
Their message received within your heart.

Seen by us with eyes of wonder,
These gossamer beings come from
yonder,
Guardian, guides, there to share
Our worries and troubles to ease the care.
To lead us to light
Visiting us in the silence of night.

A Poem Is Born

Like a whisper on the breeze,
Ephemeral as a wisp of cloud,
It teases my thoughts;
Creeping into the midnight darkness,
Catching me unawares.

Like fallen leaves blowing
Across a dusty path,
Creating patterns of colour and light;
Words forming,
Syllable by syllable,
Changing, re-arranging.

Like crumbs of cake on a plate,
Teasing and tempting,
Putting the icing on the top,
The cherry to reel me in
And give the gift of completion.

Until with a sure and steady certainty,
They find their own inimitable design,
And a poem is born to the page.
Existing as a unique entity.
A thing that never was,
And yet, it has always been.

A Fox

A flick of colour,
A whisper in the weeds.
A trick of the eye?
Deceiving the sight?

But no, a musty tang
And there! Streaming like a ruddy light
Across the wheat field, he speeds,
Master of secrecy and flight.

A Moment of Magic

A turn of the head,
Eye catches the eye,
And time stretches into eternity,
Points of elasticity, expanding, stillness.
A moment of deep understanding passes,
Extremes reached, time snaps back,
And the dog, my lifelong loyal friend,
Does it's silence bidding?

Follow Your Heart

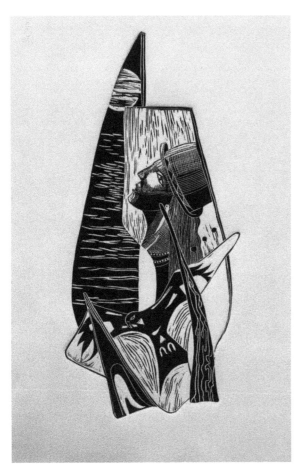

The sound of the drum, whistle and rattle,
Draw me to peace, not to the battle,
Far from a world full of care
To worlds unseen yet truly there.

Beyond the veil of a blinkered mind,
Conditioned by thoughts to keep us blind.
Wonders and wisdom to be found.
Just follow the drum, whistle and rattle,
Follow your heart beyond the battle.

The Truth in My Heart

How cool is this?
Seventy years old,
New journeys to begin
New secrets to unfold.

Now don't get me wrong
Let's not pretend
That spirit and fairy
Haven't ALWAYS been my friends.

Embraced as a child
Then hidden away
Tucked coyly inside for another day.
Patiently waiting for me to own
The wonders and knowledge
I have been shown.

Healing and yoga are always my thing
Til life caused me to change,
Afraid to be myself and sing
The truth in my heart just tucked away
Perception of normal the thought of the day.

Four In the Morning

Four in the morning
And my world sleeps quietly.
When from beyond the veil of time and
space
Drifts a vision of a slumbering face,
Amid furs and blankets, oh so worn,
For an instant, the fragile veil is torn.

Who is real, she or I?
Or do we side-by-side exist
Parted only by dimensional mist?
It comes to me in a blinding flash!

Don't you see?

She is me!

Time and Space

Side by side, we walk,
Separated by time and space.
Unseen, unknown, unable to share
The wisdom, the teachings which come from 'out there'.

Intentions are set, the veil dissolves.
The wonders are there for us to behold.
Outside of time, we meet face-to-face.
Aeons of construct tear down, accessing the
space.

Two lives, one moon, two sides of one coin,
Here, between veils, it is possible to join.
To see, to speak, to hear, to listen.
To share in one another's vision.

Here, time has no limits, no beginning, no end.
Days into minutes, allowed to bend.
Creatures commune, their knowledge to share
From rock to tree, from bird to bear.

A privilege it is to share the moon,
The sun, the stars, the elements in tune.
Side by side, we walk face to face
Connected by the web of time and space.

Age Upon Her Face

'Neath laden boughs she sits,
Shadowed from the angry sun.
Trembling the fragile leaves, flits
Breeze, playing, having fun.

Age upon her face is wise,
An Elder whose life is stoically borne,
Her soul shining through her eyes
Wrapped in wrinkles, proudly worn.

34

The Element of Air

Caressing the skin, soft and warm,
Gently blowing in the rain to the waiting corn.

Lifting skirts, frolicking with glee,
Eddying sand, stinging the knee.

Playful it seems, but then in a mood
Wrenching leaves, unsuspecting torn,
Breaking down branches old and worn.

Whipping up spray to slap the face,
Billowing sails as it gathers pace.
Holding back tides, impossible it seems,
Bow to its' strength, it's whims as it screams
Across deserts and forests, cities and spires.
Havoc and chaos and fear it inspires.
Wreaking vengeance on those who dare to exist
In the path of its' fury, its' mighty fist.

Benevolent at last, its dying sighs,
The monster retreats as its strength expires.
Life-giving force, air so rich with scent
Fickle and fierce, gentleness meant.
Cleansing and vital, the element of air,
Slumbering now in its' invisible lair.

Among The Buttercups

Shiny, waxen globes of gold,
Nod, a welcome across the fold
Deep within the meadow,
No place here for Mums and Dads so OLD!

Flying with the butterflies,
Sliding down petals glossy sides,
Leap-frogging so high, you touch the skies,
No miracle too great in their starry eyes.

Long balmy days of summer,
Tadpoles and caterpillars there to discover,
And the golden glow all around; 'Do you like
butter?'
Chucked under the chin, a child might tease
another.

So common, unheeded, natural yellow holiday
clothes,
Symbol of children nodding in the groves,
The simple flower everyone knows.

Palo Santo

Have you ever had a dream which turned into something real and tangible? Just thinking about it now gives me goosebumps.

In my dream, i was in a deep valley between the highest mountains, rugged, raw, with snow right at the top. Amongst the trees and brush was an ancient lady wearing a brightly striped skirt and a straw hat tied on around her ears with a scarf. Old and wrinkled, her name was Tipo.

I asked her what she was doing, to which she replied that she was collecting herbs and aromatics for healing. She looked at me with a bright, piercing gaze - 'You are in need of some healing', she said and reached out to me. Instantly, I felt a sort of scraping in my stomach area - then awoke abruptly, coughing and coughing for dear life.

As I awoke, I heard a name whispered in my head- Palo Santo - where had I heard that before? Then I remembered, 'Ah, an aromatherapy oil.'

I lay back and thought, 'Oh, I'll look that up in the morning', but no, something insisted.

As someone who ran an aromatherapy clinic a long time ago, I have upwards of 40 or 50 tiny bottles of oil stored in my bathroom cupboard and this one had not been out for so long that I had forgotten it. However, I crept along in the dark - so as not to awaken anyone else, and turned up the brightness on my screen to see.

I opened the cupboard door and aimed the light and there in the centre of the front row - yes! - Palo Santo. Well, I nearly fell over, how on earth did it get there?

I carefully put a drop into my palm, dabbed a little on my third eye, throat and heart, then breathed the rest in, went back to bed and instantly back into my dream.

Tipo was waiting, she smiled, and as she did, a tall person appeared with a disc like the sun for a face, the light was so powerful I could barely focus upon it and must admit I was more than a little overawed; the golden light poured into me like a warm liquid filling my veins, overspilling into my energies. I can't really explain how it felt except that it filled me with such joy that I didn't want it to end; I slept.

Now, more amazement. In the morning, I reached for a volume - Sacred Oils by Felicity Warner - and there was Palo Santo. And guess what? You'll barely believe – this particular oil comes from the heartwood of a tree that grows in Ecuador and the Galapagos Islands, which my husband and I have visited. It is also called the Incense or Holy Tree and has been used by South American Shamans from time immemorial and was revered by the Incas, who worshipped it as a sun god, Inti, with a golden disc for a face!! Oh, my word!

I am heavily into ancient civilisations and also shamanism and having visited the area years ago, it almost reduced me to tears, I know how powerful our thoughts and dreams are, but this just blew me away. On a physical level, Palo Santo helps immunity, amongst other things, but also, on an etheric level, it grounds and protects us and shows us our life purpose.

Needless to say, I am continuing to use it! So what a dream and what an outcome - follow your dreams indeed.

These two prints are the first response to this dream, but who knows what else may arise from this wonderful aromatic oil, I can't wait to follow my instincts and find out.

Woven Worlds Of Words

As a spider spins its 'silken thread
With pen and ink from a spinaret head;
We reel with such a delicate twine,
Thoughts wrought so tender, line by line.

As a skein being wound around the thumbs
The words begin to evolve
Like neatly joined thrums.

But enough for now, I need to rest,
Give relief to my weary breast
From which the thoughts I need to wrest;
In the morrow, I will be fitted best
To get these words off my chest.

But sleep eludes me,
Letters and words keep tumbling
Like fireflies out of the darkness.
I pick up my pen,
I am awake again.

The sprites in my brain
Are at it again,
In overtime, I think,
Demanding yet more pen and ink.

Now, they begin to work their magic,
Spinning, twisting, plying their threads;
Pausing awhile to add a trick,
Faces, places, joyous and tragic.

Warping and wefting ideas together,
Woven worlds of words appearing,
Bringing to life our inner dreaming,
With joyous abandon, regardless of size and shape.

Weaving a palette of words so wondrous,
A design of unique and delightful flow,
Reason and rhyme from beneath the chaos,
A cloth of words begins to grow.

Behind Closed Eyelids

Behind closed eyelids,
Sight momentarily obsolete
Starbursts of energy
Send arrows of strength
Down through rooted feet.

Twining into the darkness,
Hungry, searching for fronds
Gathering force from elements pure
To re-emerge in our vibration,
Completion in our earthly bonds.

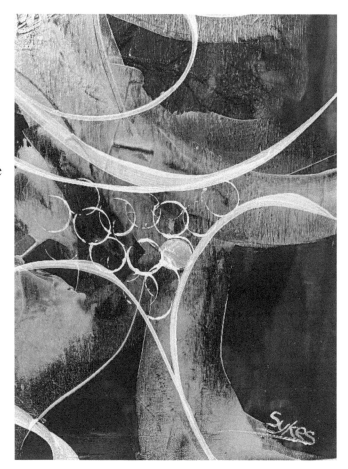

Hushness

Hushness,
Waiting.

Pulsing,
Beating,
Fingertips heating,
Palms glowing
Heavy with the weight of the sun.

Tendrils creeping, misty tweaking,
Turning liquid, smooth and flowing,
Urging with greater insistence,
Latent muscles to bend and extend.

Unfurling-like banners,
Released from restraint.

Stillness,
Waiting,
Lending,
Bending,
Body extending
In time and tune
With the music of the soul.

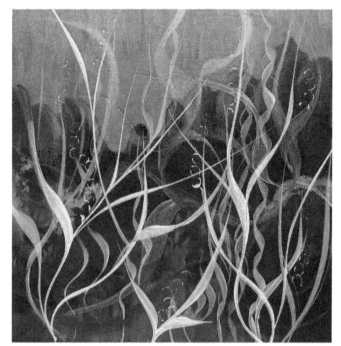

Autumn On the Hills

Crimson pinks, burnt orange yellows,
All imposed upon a skeletal framework
Of tissue-like delicacy.
Silent tinkling of golden-edged leaves
Brushed by mornings 'fairy breath.

The running of horses,
Tracks in the dew-laden grass,
Ponies imbued with the roseate light,
Glinting golden as they take flight
From who knows what imagined terror.

Lines of gracefulness, echoing form,
Subtle as the surrounding hills,
Leaving the viewer to gasp with delight
In the crispness of the autumn dawn.

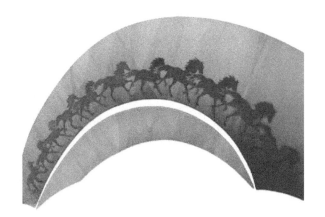

Buzzard

She sits, seemingly inert,
Atop a convenient perch
Belied only by the beady
An ever-watchful eye.
Stillness, silence, awaiting her prey.
Lifting, without warning,
Launching into the sky.

Flap, a feather twitches here,
Flap, the tail aligns there,
Float, as tho 'the winds of time
Flowed beneath her wings,
Spiralling her up and up,
Until, like a mote of dust in the void
She and the cerulean merge without sight.

Unerring, seeming laziness of flight,
Belied by the agile eye
And the sudden, startling, twisting,
Turn of speed,
Dropping like a stone.

Encounter In the Night

The softest ruffle of the skin.
A fleeting glimpse of worlds within.
The faintest whiff of your favourite perfume,
Permeates the air within the room.

Across the years, the liminal space
Dissolves across time and place.
As real to me as flesh and bone,
Felling as though I have come home.

Your warm embrace enfolding me.
A brief moment, yet memories eternal;
Never changing, never raging,
I hold you in the vastness of my heart.

Cherished memories polished bright,
By our encounter in the night.

Forever In My Heart

Doth I not grieve
Whose face is not riven
By tracks of the tears thus given?

A soul for such a brief while once lent
To light our lives,
Whose name now whispered case hurt doth
rent
A hole so jagged in the fragile garment
Of shimmering memories woven so fine,
More and more precious with the passing of
time.
A cloth of gold so tenderly wrapped,
Gossamer armour, my wounds to shield.

So judge me not by what you see,
Inside this shell is a gut-wrenched ME.
And tucked deep inside is the vital spark
Of you, forever in my heart.

Tomorrow a snowdrop,
In the summer, a red rose,
Thorns of thought will draw blood, I suppose.
But anguish and pain will one day relent,
With a smile, you'll remember the tears
you've all spent.

Gateways

Gateways to worlds as yet unknown
Portals, lintels, holes in stone.
Doorways to knowledge,
Caves to the underworld,
Archways to light,
Wonderful weave worlds where dreams can
take flight.

Worlds of ether where loved ones roam,
Waiting with patience for us to come home.
A world without prejudices, spite or hate
Which can only be accessed through our own
special gate.

Gliding, Sliding

Gliding, sliding,
Silently riding,
The slipstream of the sky.

Drift, drift,
Above the pink sea thrift,
Effortlessly twisting, turning, swooping,
The acrobat of the sky.

Undying Love

The softest of flesh,
The prettiest of lace,
Skin as soft as silk to the touch,
To run your hands
O'er treasures such as mine;
Will it ever be enough?

The softest of flesh,
The kindness of face,
All tempered from within with love,
To cast my eyes,
O'er treasures such as yours;
Can I ever give enough?

The softest of flesh,
The slowest of pace,
Years developed with friendship and
love,
To share the bonds
Of such happiness as ours;
We will always have enough.

Of Lost Love

In the loneliness of a heartbeat
A distant lamplight winks,
Beckoning us on like a finger
Of a newly engaged diamond ring.
Speaking of love, of life, of death,
Of fire and hearth and home.

But mistimed, misused, misguided,
Draw near and lament.
That spark so briefly glimpsed,
Lie a will 'o 'the wisp barely grasped,
Vanishes, extinguished, spent.

Rain Across the Sound

Incessant drumming, tempo changing,
Shades of grey, colour muting,
Slanting, sweeping, flowing down.

Purpling rivulets, angrily rushing,
Foaming, swelling, joining the throng.

Sighing, subsiding, sated at last,
Tempo slowing, beat changing.

Bejewelled, sequinned sparkles
Upon twinkling mauves, greys and blues.

Drumming muted, decreasing, silence.

Soul Food

Hot, crumbly scones, ten minutes from the
oven,
Rich, creamy butter, melting onto the tongue.
Steaming rich sponge, made especially by your
mum,
Covered in custard to satisfy your tum.

A stroll on the sand as evening approaches.
Pink-tinged clouds were touching your
emotions
Geese flying home, calling their position,
Each takes their turn within the formation.

Carols pouring forth from voices so pure,
From children whose hearts are open and true,
Memories returning from out of the blue.
Of the magical moment you said, 'I love you.'

The Chosen One

With stealth, each pad
Precisely placed.
No sound, no movement around,
Nothing to betray his presence.

He settles into place.
Patience; time is of no essence,
Just hunger driving him on
To wait and watch and wait.

In they come, a flurry of noisy wings,
Tempted by the plump, ripe corn.
Prepared to strip, rape and pillage
The golden, proud crop.

Oblivious, they land, a juicy flock,
Unknowing, uncaring, driven on
By hunger and the need to fill the
crop.

Pupils dilate – attention fixes.
A foolish, plump candidate
Is flirting with the edges.
Hunger is about to be appeased.
He is the Chosen One.

The Velvet Trap

Reaching long, sticky fingers
Across the realms of time and myth,
Wrapping around as a mist lingers,
Tenuous bars of folklore and tradition,
Invisible restraints we barely feel.

The hold they have over the years,
Centuries of unseen rules
To which life unwittingly adheres.
Holding us within a framework of golden mesh,
Like a bird in an invisible cage,
Unable or unwilling to free the flesh.

So, the human condition
Fights for modernity,
Lashing against the traces of a velvet trap,
In all but name, a vice for eternity.

Words Have Wings?

Those pedestrian things
Which march across a piece of paper?
Or dance along
In tune to a song,
Lift you up or cast you down
Create a smile or make you frown.

How oft' has your heart filled with delight
At soft whisperings in the night,
Or imagination taken flight
At the sound of pure soaring song.

Potent, poignant, powerful,
Loving, caring, hurtful.
Caressing and soothing as a lullaby,
Words filled with love or can make you cry.
Choose words tender from the heart,
From where they'll fly true as a dart,
Winging their way with true intent,
Received by the world in the way they were
meant.

Wise words, kind words,
Considered and true,
Spontaneous, joyous
Solemn and serious,
Arriving in the dead of night,
Winged threads of golden light.
Ravelling and unravelling,
Letters arranging, tumbling down
Into my lap, jostling for my attention;

Me, me, me, give me a mention!

Poems materialise out of the ether,
Teasing and shaping into words,
Sentences made before my eyes,
Creating words to delight and surprise.
Dancing like ribbons inside my head,
Onto the notebook beside my bed.
Before the words are fully drafted.
There it is, completely crafted.

Acknowledgements

I would like to thank all those who have been instrumental in my personal and artistic development, in particular John Black, who once said to me 'Stand up and be counted - if you don't do that you might as well be dead' , he was absolutely correct and I hope that I am doing him justice. Also to my tutor Pam Keeling who said that if you came from the heart, you could never be wrong; a very valuable and long standing thought. To my many students who came to me for yoga, meditation and healing over many years. I thank you all, we learned so much together along the way.

About the Author

Born and bred in Northamptonshire, England; Annette has been writing and painting since childhood, always encouraged to be creative by her Mother and Grandmother, winning awards at school for her creative essays and poems: she has distilled so many experiences into these offerings. She taught Yoga and meditation for over 25 years and has worked in healing for most of her life. Almost anything can attract her attention, from the minutae of life to a petal in the rain, or inspirations from within. She spends part of each day out in nature, walking her black Labrador, Dexter; walking the beach whenever she can and swimming in open water when the opportunity presents itself.

Spending time with her family, which includes 6 grandchildren, a multitude of dogs, sheep, cattle and horses; is also a very important part of her busy life.

Illustration and art play a large part in her life and she has work in private collections all over the world from the USA, to England and Japan to name but a few. Her work is in the Victoria and Albert Museum in London and the Scarborough Museum under the banner of the Printmakers Council of which she has been a member for many years.

Milton Keynes UK
Ingram Content Group UK Ltd.
UKHW051808050124
435485UK00003B/67